Y0-BDB-792

The Importance
Of Being Zimmer

Also by Paul Zimmer

After the Fire
The American Zimmer
The Ancient Wars
Big Blue Train
Crossing to Sunlight: Selected Poems
Crossing to Sunlight Revisited
Earthbound Zimmer
Family Reunion: Selected and New Poems
The Great Bird of Love
Live With Animals
The Republic of Many Voices
The Ribs of Death
With Wanda: Town and Country Poems
The Zimmer Poems

The
of IMPORTANCE
BEING ZIMMER

poems

▲

PAUL ZIMMER

SETTLEMENT HOUSE

Over forty years most of these poems were originally published in journals and magazines, some of them now defunct. They appeared, some in altered forms, in the following: Black Warrior Review, Brilliant Corners, Chariton Review, Counter/Measures, Crazy Horse, Denver Quarterly, Field, Georgia Review, Gettysburg Review, Harper's, Hearse, Iowa Review, Memphis State Review, Mundus Artium, Ohio Review, Pearl, Pittsburgher, Poetry Northwest, Poetry Now, Prairie Schooner, Runes, Salamagundi, Small Towner, Swallow's Tale, Three Rivers Poetry Journal, and Yankee.

The poems were chosen from the following books: The Republic of Many Voices (October House, 1969), The Zimmer Poems (Dryad Press, 1976), With Wanda (Dryad Press, 1980), Family Reunion (University of Pittsburgh Press, 1983), The Great Bird of Love (University of Illinois Press, 1989), The Big Blue Train (University of Arkansas Press, 1993), Crossing to Sunlight (University of Georgia Press, 1996), and Crossing to Sunlight Revisited (University of Georgia Press, 2007).

A number of these poems have been widely anthologized in books published by such publishers as Bantam, Bobbs-Merrill, Houghton-Mifflin, Knopf, Milkweed, Norton, Prentice-Hall, Pushcart Press, Random House, St. Martins, Simon & Schuster, Viking, and many others. "Zimmer Imagines Heaven" *was included in the recording,* A Century of Recorded Poetry, 1888-2006 *from Rhino Records, Word Beat.*

Library of Congress
Control Number: 2010935690
Zimmer, Paul
The Importance of Being Zimmer
ISBN: 978-0-578-06070-5

First edition

Manufactured in the United States of America
Cover design by Stephanie Lee
Type setting/composition by Jocelyn Wascher
Book design/production by A. Good Man Designs, Inc.

SETTLEMENT HOUSE
www.settlementhouse.us
settlement.house@yahoo.com

2200 Wilson Blvd., Suite 102 #184
Arlington, VA 22201-3324

To Suzanne
All my love

To Merrill Leffler,
and the memory of David Way

Table of Contents

III

AN ZIMMERN

Die Linien des Lebens sind verschieden
Wie Weg sind, und wie der Berge Granzen.
Was hier wir sind, kan dort ein Gott erganzen
Mit Harmonien und ewigem Lohn Frieden.
                                    ~Friedrich Holderlin

TO ZIMMER

The lines of life are various like paths
And the mountains' utmost reaches.
What we are here, elsewhere a God completes
With harmony, enduring reward, and peace.

Preface

I began with shyness and uncertainty trying to be a poet in the early nineteen-fifties. Those were intimidating times for aspiring bards. Eliot, Auden, Frost, Bishop, Cummings, Jeffers, Moore, Pound, Williams, Stevens, Aiken, Rukeyser, Berryman, Van Doren, Roethke, Spender, Graves, MacLeish, Hayden, Plath, Hughes, Carruth, Lowell, Wright were still alive. Yeats had been dead for only a decade and a half; Dylan Thomas, Hart Crane and Wilfred Owen should still have been alive.

I had not been a successful young person, thus my first books were tentative, comprised mostly of poems about people I had made up, assigning them names like Lester, Eli, Mordecai, Wanda, Phineas, Gus, Rollo. When I offered a second book manuscript comprised mostly of these made-up persona poems to October House, the wise editor, David Way, commented, "These are very interesting, but as I read the manuscript I keep asking myself one question. Who are you--who is the poet?"

"Zimmer," I said.

"Exactly," he said--and so it went. Seven years later (1976) Merrill Leffler of Dryad Press published a small edition of a book called *The Zimmer Poems*, which went out of print in short order. Since then, I have put at least a few Zimmer poems in most of the books I published. They became a sort of creative tic, and some of my friends began to worry about my literary health. They teased me by trying to imagine titles for my next books: *A Zimmer With a View*, one of them suggested (Zimmer means "room" in German), *The Enormous Zimmer*, another proffered. *Other Voices, Other Zimmers. A Zimmer Of One's Own.* One old pal even called one evening, after he'd bolstered himself with several scotches, and said quite seriously, "You must never say the word 'Zimmer' in a poem again."

Wow! Okay, okay, okay! I did not want to be a silly boy. So I stopped for a number of years, and even published a book of poems~a pretty good book~without a single Zimmer included. But eventually I asked myself again: Who are you?

I am Zimmer, and I could no longer resist allowing this ubiquitous phantom to at least occasionally sneak into my scene again. In an effort to control myself and not be cloying, I even wrote some parodies of Zimmer poems as I imagined other famous poets would have written them ("A Zimmershire Lad," "Death of the Hired Zimmer," "Leaves of Zimmer" and others). Now, as I begin to survey my lifelong writings, I find that, amongst many others, I published more than 130 Zimmer poems over the years. Recently I laboriously gathered them all together and looked at them.

Here are less than half of these, carefully gleaned from the whole lot, including some new ones at the end. I'm too old to be shy and uncertain now. To hell with it! A pretty good book.

Quickly, I must admit that I have done just a bit of fiddling, trimming some poems slightly, performing major/minor surgery on others. By doing these revisions I do not undervalue my earlier efforts or the person I was then, but I respect these poems enough to make them as good as I can make them, to finish them as best I can~ as I am (I hope) a wiser Zimmer than I was before. Finish is a good word and process~for building furniture or houses, painting pictures, pitching a baseball, shooting films, composing music, dancing a dance, living a life and making poems.

I

ZIMMER'S HEAD THUDDING AGAINST THE BLACKBOARD

At the blackboard I had missed
Five number problems in a row,
And was about to foul a sixth
When the old, exasperated nun
Began to pound my head against
My six mistakes. When I wept,
She threw me back into my seat,
Where I hid my head and swore
That very day I'd be a poet,
And curse her yellow teeth with this.

ZIMMER GUILTY OF THE BURNT GIRL

Once a week
The burnt girl came peddling to our house,
Touching her sweet rolls with raisin fingers,
Her raw face struggling like a bubble
Through lava to say what she had
To sell and why, "Please buy my sweets
To mend my face."

Always I hid behind the piano and heard
My unflinching mother quietly buy a few,
And imagined apricots shriveling in sun,
Spiders writhing and dripping over matches.
Always, when the burnt girl had gone,
I heard my mother drop her purchase
In the rubbish to be burned and
I came out to see the pink graftings,
The horrid, sugared layers of the rolls.

I do not want
The burnt girl to come again.
I am guilty for her and of her.
Always in fever I think of that face.
Sometimes in love I believe that I am
Fire consuming myself, and the burnt girl
Suffers from my love as she sells
Her rolls to mend her face.

ZIMMER'S STREET

My street thunders like
A long chimney falling
When morning comes up.
A thousand great cars
Relentlessly flash and fume.
Trucks come, an ambulance,
A wrecking ball and crane,
Hearse, cabs, a mobile home,
Airplanes roar and stack above
My father and mother
On their way to work.

My wife and children
Play on the sidewalks,
Grandfather walks to
The bakery, my older sister
Bounces a ball till dark.
All things have come down
This street: Thanksgiving,
Christmas, victory, marriage.
It takes all day for
Pavement to stop hissing
So that I can sleep at night.

ZIMMER IN GRADE SCHOOL

In grade school I wondered
Why I had been born
To wrestle in the ashy puddles,
With my square nose
Streaming mucus and blood,
My knuckles puffed from combat
And the old nun's ruler.
I feared everything: God,
Learning, and my schoolmates.
I could not count, spell or read.
My report card proclaimed
These scarlet failures.
My parents wrung their loving hands.
My guardian angel wept constantly.

But I could never hide anything.
If I peed my pants in class
The puddle was always quickly evident,
My worst mistakes were at
The blackboard for Jesus and all
The saints to see.
                    Even now
When I hide behind elaborate mask
It is always known that I am Zimmer,
The one who does the messy papers
And fractures all his crayons,
Who spits upon the radiators
And sits all day in shame
Outside the office of the principal.

WHAT ZIMMER WOULD BE

When asked, I used to say,
"I want to be a doctor."
Which is the same thing
As a child saying,
"I want to be a priest,"
Or
"I want to be a magician,"
Which is the laying on
Of hands, the vibrations,
The rabbit in the hat,
Or the body in the cup,
The curing of the sick,
And the raising of the dead.

"Fix and fix, you're all better,"
I would say
To the neighborhood wounded
As we fought the world war
Through the vacant lots of Ohio.
"Fix and fix, you're all better."
And they would rise
To fight again.
                    But then
I saw my aunt die slowly of cancer,
And a man struck down by a car.

All along I had really
Wanted to be a poet,
Which is, you see, almost
The same thing as saying,

"I want to be a priest.
I want to be a doctor."
Or
"I want to be a magician."
All along, without realizing it,
I had wanted to be a poet.

Fix and fix, you're all better.

THE DAY ZIMMER LOST RELIGION

The first Sunday I missed Mass on purpose
I waited all day for Christ to climb down
Like a wiry flyweight from the cross and
Club me on my irreverent teeth, to wade into
My blasphemous gut and drop me like a
Red hot thurible, the devil roaring in
Reserved seats until he got the hiccups.

It was a long cold way from the old days
When cassocked and surpliced I mumbled Latin
At the old priest and rang his obscure bell.
A long way from the dirty wind that blew
Soot like venial sins across the school yard
Where God reigned as a threatening
One-eyed triangle high in the fleecy sky.

The first Sunday I missed Mass on purpose
I waited all day for Christ to climb down
Like the playground bully, the cuts and mice
Upon his face agleam, and pound me
Till my irreligious tongue hung out.
But of course He never came, knowing that
I was grown up and ready for him now.

ONE FOR THE LADIES AT THE TROY LAUNDRY, WHO COOLED THEMSELVES FOR ZIMMER

The ladies at the Troy Laundry pressed
And pressed in the warm fog of their labor.
They cooled themselves at the windows,
Steam rising from their gibbous skins
As I dawdled home from school.
In warmer weather they wore no blouses,
And if I fought the crumbling coke pile
To the top, they laughed and waved
At me, billowy from their irons.

Oh man, the ladies at the Troy Laundry
Smelled like cod fish out of water,
And yet the very fur within their armpits
Made me rise wondering and small.

WANDA AND ZIMMER

Wanda, my pussy willow, cupcake,
My chinchilla red rabbit,
I wanted to love you so much,
To chase you into corners and
Pet you till your ears lay down,
Till the membranes drew back
From over your rosy eyes;
I wanted to make you breathe easily,
But you didn't love me,
Ran like hell when you saw me,
Flicked up your fine, hind legs
When I came near and pissed
On my pant legs.
                          Wanda, I was
Always afraid to break you,
But still you were frightened
Of my fingers, teeth and groin,
Certain that if I held you
Your small bones would bend
And crack off one another,
Your organs crush together
In the agony of my affection.

A Zimmershire Lad

Oh what a lad was Zimmer
    Who would rather swill than think,
Who grew to fat from trimmer
    While taking ale to drink.

Now his stomach hangs so low,
    And now his belt won't hook,
Now his cheeks go to and fro
    When he leaps across a brook.

Oh lads, ere your flesh decay,
    And your sight grows dimmer,
Beware the ale foam in your way
    Or you will end like Zimmer.

ZIMMER, THE LUCKLESS ICE FISHERMAN

For two days I gazed down lines
Through a cold, rectangular hole
I had chopped through the ice,
But my avid fingers felt only
Suffering of bait upon my hooks,
And slow shifting of currents.
No bites, no bites.

Hard wind punished me,
The cracking of ice became
Thunder that frightened me.

At night in the lodge I dreamt
The transom above my door was
A hole in ice and I was a fish
Flicking through cold darkness,
Ignoring Zimmer's lines,
All the cursing that he gave his luck
Above me, all his ranting and sucking
At his whiskey bottle.
                                    I had but
One thought repeating in my cold,
Silvery brain:
Zimmer does not deserve me.
Zimmer does not deserve me.

JULIAN BARELY MISSES ZIMMER'S BRAINS

As we were hunting over
Snowy fields, Julian
Slipped on a viscid clod,
And his shotgun cracked
Both barrels past my ear.

I sat down on a cold stone
To feel my chubby brains
Float down like stuffing from
Old cushions, my face rammed
Back through the grinder
Of my teeth. Crows arrived
To fork me apart like tender meat.

But I was still alive with
The sense that I was still alive.
Whitetails hurdled in tall grass,
Rabbits scurried into thistle,
And ducks applauded overhead.

ZIMMER, THE DRUGSTORE COWBOY

Some days I am strangely empty, as if
I'd been stunned by a concrete tit at birth,
Dull as a penny bouncing off a cinder block;
My white socks down over high tops,
Big lugs heavy with gravel and mud.

I get up in the early morning,
Sit on a drugstore bench in the mist,
Drink Dr. Peppers for breakfast until
The boys at the Shell station start
Revving motors like a pride of lions.
I wait all day for things to cool down,
Watch bread trucks and big rigs
Deliver and depart, pass out of sight
Down the interstate.
                        I get mad about things:
Shattered safety glass in the streets,
Stupid heat lightning swelling out of trees,
Groove, gash, dent, dog, mosquito, fly~
Once in a while something just froths me,
Anger bursting through my skin and slapping
Surface like a the side of a bluegill,
My cold, bony mouth snapping and sucking
At hot air, my eyeballs pivoting
Until I can settle myself again.

At night I wander the town, look up
Through tiny squares of window screens,
Inside squares of pictures and doorframes,
Inside glowing squares of television,

Inside squares of windows.
Everything is plumb and solid in the night,
Corners of lamplight fastening things down.

Wherever I move, darkness moves,
Because I am my own shadow.
Crickets tinker with silence.
I walk in dusky alleys, see stars
Well out of the roofs of buildings,
Swarming to multiply like a mass
Of tiny gnats in my gaze. I wonder,
How many stars could I see if I watched forever?
Star growing into star, year after year,
New revelations spreading beyond sight,
Massing until they all grow together,
Swelling like heat lightning out of trees.

Then maybe I could live like a bluegill
All of the time, full of hunger and purpose,
Cool, trim, quick in the water,
One little muscle waiting to strike.

SUZIE'S ENZYME POEM

What a drag it must be for you!
I slog along, ignoring you like my heart beat.
I gurgle and mold like an old fruit cellar;
Then suddenly you'll walk through a door
And foam me up like ancient cider in heat.
Then I'll fall all about you, blathering
With lost time, making you numb with words,
Wanting to mix our molecules, trying
To tell you of weeks in fifteen minutes.
Sometimes you must wonder what the hell
It is with Zimmer.
                        This is to tell you
That you are my enzymes, my yeast,
All the things that make my cork go pop.

ZIMMER ENVYING ELEPHANTS

I have a wide, friendly face
Like theirs, yet I can't hang
My nose like a fractured arm
Nor flap my dishpan ears.
I can't curl my canine teeth,
Swing my tail like a filthy tassel,
Nor make thunder without lightning.

But I'd like to thud amply around
For a hundred years or more,
Stuffing an occasional tree top
Into my mouth, screwing hugely for
Hours at a time, gaining weight,
And slowly growing a few hairs.

Once in a while I'd charge a power pole
Or smash a wall down just to keep
Everybody loose and at a distance.

ZIMMER DRUNK AND ALONE, DREAMING
OF OLD FOOTBALL GAMES

I threw the inside of my gizzard out, splashing
Down the steps of that dark football stadium
Where I had gone to celebrate the ancient games.
But I had been gut-blocked and cut down by
A two-ton guard in one quarter of my fifth.
Fireflies broke and smeared across my eyes,
And the half-moon spiraled on my corneas.
Between spasms, crickets beat halftime to
My tympanum, and stars twirled like fire batons
Inside the darkness.
                          The small roll at my gut's end,
Rising like a cheer, curled up intestines to my stomach,
Quaking to my gullet, and out my tongue again.
Out came old victories, defeats and scoreless ties,
Out came three-quarters of my fifth,
Until exhausted, my wind gone and teeth sour,
I climbed the high fence out of that dark stadium,
Still smarting from booing and hard scrimmage.
I zigzagged down the street, stiff-arming buildings,
And giving flashy hip fakes to the lamp posts.
I cut for home, a veteran broken field drunkard,
With my bottle tucked up high away from fumbles.

ZIMMER IMAGINES HIMSELF BEING
POET-IN-RESIDENCE

There is so much to look forward to:
I will reside in a house that is chanted,
In rooms that are quoted by echoes.
The faucets will run with metaphor,
And toilets will flush down prose.
Beds will be for headlong dreaming,
And all flat surfaces will spell
The purest and most honest sentences.

I will not eat or drink in the residence;
My veins will flood with art and truth.
Outdoors, sunlight will flash and bend enchanted,
Rain will break it down to purest colors.
Students will ask, "Who resides in that house?"
And the wind and stars will answer, "Zimmer."

ZIMMER LOATHING THE GENTRY

Their faces are like fine watches
Insinuating jewels.
Their movements can buy or sell you.
When the legs of gentry dance for charity,
Meat splashes in the soups of the poor.
The eyes of gentry are polished and blown.
When they look at you, you are worthless.
The gentry protect their names like hymens,
They suck their names like thumbs;
But they sign their names and something happens,
While, Zimmer, I can write Zimmer
All day, and nothing happens.

ZIMMER FINDS IMBELLIS IN THE ANCIENT GRAVES

I had not expected to find him here,
Gnarled like blackened dung
In the low tranquility of the bog
Amongst shattered swords and caltrops,
This Imbellis, who was dealt out
Cell-by-cell a thousand years ago
To calcium and ancient gods.

How long can a nightmare last?
I see his lips pulled back from his teeth,
Whiskers fringed about his jagged scars,
Brow coved over his antique anger.
My balls clutch and rise,
And I hold my arms high
To parry his blows.

I remember his havoc,
Feel it rising from clods again,
Uncoiling like a spring
To knock me skittering into
A double vision of darkness.

ZIMMER RECEIVES THE DICTIONARY OF SYMBOLS

How do I recover from
The dictionary of symbols?
Rose, rod, marvelous rood,
Skull, claw, terrible scythe.
Suddenly I am all symbols:
Slight crook of my spine,
Cauldron of my mouth,
Bramble of my hair,
Scroll of my tongue,
Mandalas of my fingertips.
I am so much, mean so much.

Now I respect all marks
And executed yearnings:
Moon holes in old bones,
Notches of worms in wood,
Dance marks of the bee,
Rings, rattles, well-worn paths,
Rain slant, grooves and ruts,
Scratch marks of this pen;
Symbol of habit, habit of symbols,
And the striving of all disorder.

ORGANIC FORM AND FINAL MEANING
IN THE PLUMED ZIMMER

Zimmer represents the whispering of the cosmos;
The universe grows out from his belly button,
And his nebulae and gases are serious heat.
Zimmer inculcates an arrant subjectivism
Which indicates that, though crudely realized,
He means well, impressing with his keen sense of tension.
Yet he is the simple archetype of satisfaction.
One notes that his moustache points at his ears,
Representing his most secret desire to be
An elephant. Though Zimmer is unlettered,
He is no native genius. He wishes very much
That Francis Bacon had written his poems.
Permit me one final definitive statement:
Zimmer does not mean. He is.

ZUMER IS ICUMEN IN

Zumer is icumen in,
Lewdly sing whohoo;
Floweth hed and gloweth red
And bringth the nuhdie too.
Sing whohoo!
Owlhe bloteth after ram,
Druleth over calfe cu
Bumper riseth, butte sizeth;
More he sing whohoo.
Whohoo   Whohoo!
Wel sing whohoo nu!
Sing whohoo nu! Sing whohoo!
Sing whohoo
Nu!

ZIMMER'S BED

Old bed, you are a garden.
Each night I roll over
And sink through you
Like a root into
Darkness. Now I will
Say, goodnight, goodnight.
I have slept on you
So long I forget
How much I love you.
Yet my children and poems
Are sewn in you.
Can you tell me
If they will bloom
And be immortal?
Never mind. Goodnight,
Goodnight.

II

DEAR WANDA,

Last night I dreamt you were Emily Dickinson.
I waited for you, uneasy in your parlor.
After many hours you came into the room.
You were ill, your temples sunken,
Light sweat stippled your upper lip.
You made me nervous. You handed
This poem to me and left again:

This was my letter to a Moor-
Writ in mad divinest sense-
From a life closed twice before
That made my lines so lean and tense

The words I chose were hard and few-
Of liquor, heather, snake and claw-
Of other things I never knew
And did not see-but saw

Wanda, I have remembered
Every line. The cadence has
Frightened me, the rhymes leer
At my uneasiness. Please, do not
Come into my dreams again.
                    Love
                    Zimmer

THE GAMES IN THE FIELD

It took us two days in heat to mow
The hay down in the field and rake it
Away in preparation for our games.

When we'd set the bounds at last,
Wanda stood solemnly with squirrels
And deer to watch us from the trees.

Eli plunged in the circles and squares,
Julian dashed, Cecil dove at the ball,
Zimmer shouted his taunts and threats
As we tore and strained against each other
To show our broken, bloody plumage.

As always, when it was over,
And results were duly recorded,
Wanda slipped away from us all,
Not caring for our achievements
And keeping her choice to herself.

WANDA AND ZIMMER IN THE TENDERLOIN

That tenderloin apartment building
Smelled of urine and was sore
As a gum boil.
                            Its heat pipes clanked
All night, its toilets groaned.
Its tenants were berserk or in despair.

The old place ran like a canker,
Its plaster festering in its lath,
Cold bricks seeping a bile,
Filthy shadows scurried for corners
Each time we opened a drawer.

But we flew in like two spring robins
To build our nest in that rotting elm,
Tucking in cellophane, tinsel, new twigs.

We conjured the elevator upstairs again,
Beckoned sunshine down the air shaft,
Loved the moon through the grimy window.

ZIMMER'S LAST GIG

Listening to hard bop,
I stayed up all night
Just like good times.
I broke the old waxes
After I'd played them:
Out of Nowhere, Mohawk,
Star Eyes, Salt Peanuts,
Confirmation, one-by-one;
Bird, Bean, Bud, Brute, Pres,
All dead, all dead anyway
As clay around my feet.

Years ago I'd wanted to
Take Wanda to Birdland,
Certain that the music
Would make her desire me,
That after a few sets
She would submit to
Rhythm and sophistication.
Then we could slip off
Into the wee hours with
Gin, chase, and maryjane,
Check into a downtown pad,
Do some fancy jitterbugging
Between the lilywhites.

But Wanda was no quail.
Bud could have passed
Out over the keys,
Bird could have shot
Up right on stage,

Wanda would have missed
The legends. The band
Could have riffed
All night right by
Her ear, she never
Would have bounced.

ZIMMER AND THE GHOST

We are like the anguished masters of a lost dog,
Suddenly remembering all the sweet things
That she was. Wanda is dead now and
None of us really knew who she was.

She was the best of us,
Always had the courage to depart,
To frighten us by moving beyond bounds.
But now she has gone too far.
She will not come to us again.

Yesterday I thought I saw a ghost in
The strangled light of the ancient field.
"Z i m m e r!" it lisped at me
As it fumed out of loose sod,
Its leering face a bag
Of working maggots, and its hands
And nails clacking and constricting.
"Z i m m e r!" it called.

It seemed to be an elm stump beckoning,
A fencepost or a buckthorn blowing,
Even as I hoped that it was Wanda.
But as I walked toward it, my left eye
Twitched, my fingertips froze,
And my heart rammed the inside
Of my ribs.

It was nothing but mist, of course;
But I had wanted it to be Wanda,
Had wanted to be baffled once again!

Wanda! When I am a ghostly spirit
Rising wormy and long-buried to walk
The earth again, I'll never toy as you do
With my victims, nor simply be a flicker
In the corner of their frightened eyes;
But I will rise up in all my pearly,
Frozen essence, grinding my snags,
And moaning like an albino walrus.
I will look my victim squarely under
Her sweating eyebrows, and ask,
    "D o   y o u   l o v e   m e?"
And if she answers yes, then~
And only then~will I fade.

When Angels Came to Zimmer

One morning a great gaggle slid
Down through holes in clouds,
Twirling like maple seeds through
Branches to my window-screen.

Fervent as new tussock moths,
They flapped and dashed themselves,
Smearing their heavenly dust,
Until Zimmer, in pity and alarm,
Opened to let them into his study.

They flew in with smiles and sighs,
Making him bashful, as if a dozen
Gorgeous chorus girls had suddenly
Pranced into the room.
                          They perched on
Bookshelves, cigar stubs, and beer cans;
One even tried to sit on Zimmer's lap.

All day they danced the Lindy,
And some, not knowing better, dabbled
Their darling toes in the toilet bowl.

They sang chorus after chorus of
Stardust and *Moonlight in Vermont*,
Constantly touching and stroking Zimmer.
Then at day's end, as if someone
Had rung a bell, they stood to sing
A final chorus of *Deep Purple*.

With a whoosh of air and expensive perfume,
They fluttered from the room and ascended.
Zimmer stepped out to watch them rise
And flapped his dirty hankie at the stars.

Two Drinking Songs

1. Zimmer Repudiates Beer

It is an idiot's way to die,
Therefore when you next see me
I will look like a cactus needle
Sans body, liquid, and weight,
But keen enough to make you pay.
No more will I raise the glass
And swallow till I see the froth.
I swear by the Muse that I will
Cease this slaughtering of brain cells,
Will no longer build this stomach
Brick by brick and glass by glass
Until the lights grow dim.
Though in summer it cools me
And in winter it warms my soul,
I herewith deny this perfection.

2. Zimmer Resists Temperance

Some people view life as food served
By a psychopath. They do not trust it.
But Zimmer expects always to be happy.
Puzzled by melancholy, he pours a reward
And loves this world relentlessly.

The vessels in his nose begin to glow.
Each day he plans to end up squatting like
Gandhi with a glass of unsweetened tea.
He wishes he looked like a Rouault Christ.
Yet who says Zimmer should not compensate himself?

Someday he may fall face down

In the spew of his own buoyancy,
But while the world and his body
Are breaking down,
Zimmer will hold his glass up.

LEAVES OF ZIMMER

You Zimmer! Whimpering, heavy, mumbling, lewd:
Does America sing you a sad song?
It is a trifle! Resign yourself!
Nothing is without flaw.
Confess that you feel small buds unclutching again!
Confess that the rich sod turns up to you always
    as your lover!
By God! Accept nothing less than this for affection:
Stars dangling like green apples on distant peaks:
Sea foam combing itself through rocks:
No foofoo can strip you of this!
No mountebanks can take it away!
If one is deprived, then all are deprived:
America will love us all, or it will not love.
Camerado! Give me your hand.
All of us will go! Boatmen and trappers,
Bridegroom and bride, sailors and drifters,
Woodsmen, mechanics, preachers, lawyers, fishermen.
We must also raise the insulted and injured.
Even the president will come!
If one of us falls, the others must wait:
For lacking one, we lack all.
Camerado! My left hand hooks you round the waist,
My right hand points to America.
Let us feel the country under our boot-soles:
Let us seek it in the air we breathe.

IMBELLIS AT ZIMMER'S WINDOW

Something came to my window last night
And looked in when I couldn't look out:
Enormous footprints in the dew,
Broken circles of spider webs,
Hair mats in berry bushes,
Piles of steaming turds and
Drool stains on the windowsill.

Along the roads there are damage reports:
Chickens throttled, sundered dogs and cats,
Uprooted trees and broken pottery.
Something got into a barn and set it afire.
Evidence leads down the pathway to my window.
There are claw marks on the sash.

Will he remember what he saw?
Will he come again?
Should I try somehow to improve myself?

Zimmer Sees Imbellis Rise from the Water

Brothers, sisters, I have seen the enemy.
I could not explain sudden boiling of surface,
Fish leaping as my boat rocked in frigid waters,
A huge, refracted shadow in the water,
Plucking and snapping at my deep lines.

Then there was lepered skunk on the wind
And I felt his spleeny gaze on me,
Saw that half-mortified son-of-a-bitch
Sneaking and sliding on shore,
Hideous angles and ruddy flesh,
His eyes streaming like infections
As he hacked and stewed at me,
Snapping off awesome obscenities.

As I rowed for shore he circled
And showed his mossy teeth.
I landed bellowing and flashing my own blade.

Oh we were something under that
Laden sky, sniffing rags and blood!
The two of us spent the whole day in a lather,
Feinting and flaring at each other.
At dusk we retreated gory, with matters
Unsettled, flinging threats over our shoulders.

Brothers, sisters, I have met Imbellis.
Everyday he ruts and strikes flint
In our dry forests, shits in the waters
Of our lakes and stalks our borders.
We can do nothing but stand together.

ZIMMER REMEMBERS RELIGION

I wanted God to come down like an anvil
Through the fan vaulting of the chancel,
And smash the lofted chalice, precious blood
Dousing the upraised face of Father Animus.
I wanted tangible relics~bones, teeth, splinters,
Confirmed reports of prophets in the country,
The sky and sea each day to open and slam shut,
Sun veering, mountains rolling to bury Imbellis.

I wanted holy and powerful signs. Instead,
I got the mystic drone of Father Animus,
Waft of noxious incense in the nave,
Sermons full of platitude and caveat,
A feckless Host, no more than a symbol,
Self-righteous glad-handing in the vestibule.

Despite all glorying and posturing, I say still
That God must also be in mud and corruption.
He made this world and He is of it all:
Piddle of flies, the grit between one's teeth.
He nestles not only in flutings and flower cups,
But He is in scum, dry rot, invective, war,
He is utmost kindness, yet bewildering neglect.

THE NEWS OF THE DAY

The voice of our leaders is the sound
Of water overwhelming us,
Cruelty of fire discovering tinder,
Thud of boulders after a long fall.

The voice of Zimmer
Is the hiss of smoke from sapwood,
Fidget of mice in weeds,
Any rain that falls on the roof.

This is the news of the day:
Ill winds drubbing the government,
Rebellions pulverized in distant countries,
Threats and howling at our borders,
Armies lacing up for war.

This is the news of Zimmer:
His breakfast egg was spotted,
Today his bowels were airy,
A bed spring creaked as he slept,
Three of his words fell into place.

ZIMMER AND THE AGE OF ZEPPELINS

There was the faint sound
Of a piano playing ragtime
And then an abrupt eclipse.
Zimmer looked up and saw the zeppelin
Like a giant okra ponderously
Sliding over the sun and through
The treetops, its girders creaking, echoing.

It took all day to pass over
As the sound of idle laughter
Drifted down from the promenade.
Zimmer heard the tinkle of
Ice and glasses from the lounge.
At dusk he watched its tail fins
Cross over into the night.

It had been such a memorable day,
Zimmer could not comprehend
A sudden astonishing fireball
And thunder over the horizon:
The end of the age of zeppelins.

He ran to see the great craft
Roaring in its own air and fire,
Bodies dropping like tent-worms
From a torched nest, and then
The whole thing down in a blazing heap,
Cries of the injured amongst the debris,
The old moon sailing on above the agony.

YELLOW SONNET

Zimmer no longer wishes to write
About the dimming of his lights,
Recounting all his small terrors.
Instead he tells of brilliance,
Walking home from first grade
In springtime, sunlight descending
To hold itself and dazzle him
In an outburst of dandelions.
It was then he learned that
He would always love yellow,
Its warm dust on his knuckles,
The memory of gathering its bits
To carry home in his lunch pail
As a love gift for his mother.

ZIMMERIUS VILISSIMUS

If I had been consulted,
This would have been a prodigious
Bird of multi-colored plumage
With a call like a freight train.
At sight of its angry, massive
Tracks in the snow, man and beast
Would have dithered with fear.

But indeed and shamefully,
It is a tiny, piss-colored bird
(formerly called a paltry tyrannulet)
Inhabiting thickets in Panama,
It hops nervously around with
Its tail half-cocked, shrieking
Peee-yip, peee-yip, peee-yip!

ZIMMER PONDERS HIS LIFE IN BOOKS

Suddenly the books fly in
Under reckless skies,
Swirling and flapping,
The inscrutable, difficult,
Excellent, insipid, insane,
As a flock of alarmed crows
Yawking and spattering.

The sky fills and breaks
As books wheel into a dive
Through roll and pitch of day,
Then slump down to sit
In the trees and brood,
Pecking their lice in the rain.

But even in this heavy weather,
In midst of their complaints,
I remember their sunlit times
And how they always come back
On the great days of my life.

ZIMMER TO HIS STUDENTS

Sometimes when you lie on your back
In an open field and gaze
Up at the sky, you imagine
It is a blank piece of paper.

Your terror rises and you fear
You will plunge out into the vast,
Blue void forever. Then you will
Find that your body yearns
To sink roots, that you can
Save yourself only by clutching
The constant tufts of grass.

Let me counsel you:
Pay attention to that which you take
For granted. Poetry comes to you
Like puberty~fervent, perplexing,
Unexpected~before you know what
Is happening. It is a humbling process,
Leading to wisdom that can preserve you.

THE DUKE ELLINGTON DREAM

Of course Zimmer was late for the gig.
Duke was pissed and growling at the piano,
But Jeep, Brute, Rex, Cat and Cootie
All moved down on the chairs
As Zimmer walked in with his tenor.
Everyone knew that the boss had arrived.

Duke slammed out the downbeat for *Caravan*
And Zimmer stood up to take his solo.
The whole joint suddenly started jiving,
Chicks came up to the bandstand
To hang their lovelies over the rail.
Duke was sweating but wouldn't smile
Through chorus after chorus after chorus.

It was the same with *Satin Doll,*
Do Nothing Till You Hear From Me,
Warm Valley, In a Sentimental Mood;
Zimmer blew them so they would stay played.

After the final set he packed
His horn and was heading out
When Duke came up and collared him.
"Zimmer," he said, "You most astonishing ofay!
You have shat upon my charts,
But I love you madly."

How Zimmer Will Be Reborn

Make it an ancient rookery,
A crumbling abbey in York,
A place where God's old slaves,
Cistercians, still dwell in
The spirit of dingy birds.

Make it a grizzled sky
Rolling over broken walls.
Make the air chill and wet,
Desire for warmth overwhelming.

Despite the outrage
Of righteous flocks,
I will begin to claw
My way up worn stones
Toward a reechy nest
Tucked into a cranny.

When the mother rook
Goes off to forage I'll
Slip into the pocket
Of moldy leaves and sticks,
And snuggle down
Amongst her ticking eggs.

When she returns I'll
Listen to her tender croaks,
Feel myself being coaxed
By the song of woman;
The desire to come forth
Overwhelming, to rise,
Guard my few square yards,
To strut and screech
At anything that moves.

THE GREAT BIRD OF LOVE

I want to become a great night bird
Called The Zimmer, grow intricate gears
And tendons, brace my wings on updrafts,
Roll them down with a motion
That lifts me slowly into the stars
To fly above the troubles of the land.

When I soar the moon will shine past
My shoulder and slide through
Streams like a luminous fish.
I want my cry to be huge and melancholy,
The undefiled movement of my wings
To fold and unfold on rising gloom.

People will see my silhouette from
Their windows and be comforted,
Knowing that, though oppressed,
They are cherished and watched over,
Can turn to kiss their children,
Tuck them into their beds and say:
       Sleep tight.
       No harm tonight,
       In starry skies
       The Zimmer flies.

III

ZIMMER CLOSES HIS FAMILY HOME

How quickly old times empty,
Load after load~seventy years
Hauled out in a day until
Each corner has been violated.

Now home is not where I go,
But where I came from;
It is the simple space around my body,
The very layers of my skin.

ZIMMER WARNS HIMSELF AGAINST OLD AGE

Well, Zimmer, old reeking cricket,
There you go sliding your galoshes
Along cement as dismal and
Hard as your petrified bowels,
Your hands like frayed moths
Raising a yellow snot rag
To your swampy nostrils.
With your eyes unplugged now
Behind fly-specked spectacles,
Knees squawking, elbows flaring,
Joints burning, penis trickling,
Feet dead, and teeth long gone,
You pay now with mumbling for
All the money you never saved,
And all the poems you ever wrote.

Death of the Hired Zimmer

She sat watching the moth at the candle,
Waiting for Eli. When he came home
She ran to tell him, "Zimmer is back.
I saw him step out of the woods
At noon, look both ways, then head
For our place. What can we do?"

"Be calm," Eli said. "Was he alone?"

"Only his shadow, a bulge in his pocket.
Eli, be kind," she said, and took
The market things from his arms.
"Don't laugh at him. He has a plan."

"I'll go and see him now," he said.
"You sit and watch the moon slide
Through that patch of clouds."

                    He went.
Came back, too soon, it seemed to her.
            "Dead?" she questioned
As he sat down.
            "Drunk," was all he answered.

ZIMMER LURCHES FROM CHAIR TO CHAIR

Zimmer, lurching from chair to chair,
Can count on one hand the total
Of minutes he feels good in a day.

As thunderheads muster in the west
He sees an intruder planted
Knee-deep in hovering mist
At the near edge of his north forty.

Zimmer thinks to light out after him,
But his legs and breath are gone.

What's more, this is not some
Clatter-boned spirit hovering over
The field—but a stranger standing
Firm as a knife thrust into sod.

Zimmer bravely addresses his body.
He says, Flesh, you will not be afraid,
You will not sweat and grow numb.
Bones, he says, stand firm with me.

But someone is knocking at his door,
Blowing cold air through his keyhole;
Something is turning the knob,
And fear torques Zimmer's ribs.

THE BEAST OF SOLDIERS GROVE

Had it been a hellhound?
Bigfoot come to rampage
In the woods of Wisconsin?
The county paper said
It was a "bear with its hair
Burnt off in a brush fire."

The five of us had labored
Too long at our woodcutting.
Now dusk slipped into the trees.

The bear blustered out of
A stand of stricken elms~
This sudden fury
That fell upon us,
This beast that looked
Like a wounded man~
And the moment was combustible,
Blowing apart to lodge in
Different portions of our minds.

"The stink's what I remember,"
Says Eli now. "It rose up like
A dump fire, or some high coon
Left by an owl to rot."

Lester shakes his head.
"What raised my hair
Most was that face,
Rawer than a cankered beet."

"It got a paw on me,"
Gus recollects~"cold

As a gravedigger's cock,
And yet it burned me."

"It knocked me down,"
Said Rollo, "and split
My lip. It tasted like
A nest of last year's bees."

But I remember only
The sounds it made
After we'd heaved
All our firewood at it
And were skedaddling.

I looked back to see it
Naked and suffering
In the lowering dark,
A demon potent but lost,
Declining into its pain.

"Lester," it rasped at us.
"Gus, Rollo, Eli," as if making
A list to shame us. Then,
"Zimmer," it groaned. I swear.

ZIMMER IN THE MEAD HALL
CONSIDERS THE PERCENTAGES

I have heard that Grendel   scorns all wounding weapons,
Therefore I will strongly meet him   on his own terms
With my knucklebones, fingernails   and tearing teeth.
Should the morbid monster   somehow win and still
The full-flexing of my heart,   then the crossbar
On the heavy door of this mead hall   will snap
Like a blighted bough   and he will enter frothing,
Come to masticate your muscles   and Dane bones.
And if I fail,   my full-friends, do not seek to
Tend my corpse, for the grim-goblin   will bury it
In his great maw, bursting its organs   and dying
The black sweating swamps red   with Zimmer's blood.

"ONE O'CLOCK JUMP"

Still tingling with Basie's hard cooking,
Zimmer was standing at the bar between sets
When a guy next to him ordered scotch and milk.
Zimmer looked to see who had this stray taste
And almost swooned when he saw the master.

Basie knocked back his shot, then,
When he saw this kid gaping at him,
Raised his milk chase to that peachy face
And rolled out his complete smile
Before going off with friends to
Leave Zimmer in a state of grace.

•

A year later, Zimmer was renting rooms
From a woman named Tillie, who wanted
No jazz in her dank, unhallowed house;
Objecting even to lowest volume of solo piano,
She'd puff upstairs to rat-a-tat-tat on his door.

Zimmer grew opaque and unwell,
Slouched to other apartments,
Begging to play his records.
Duked, dePrezed, and unBased,
Longing for Billie, Monk, Brute, or Zoot,
He lived in silence through
That whole lost summer.

Aware of divine favor, he bided his time
Until his last night in Tillie's godless house.
Late~when he knew she was hard asleep~
He gave her the full One O'clock Jump,

Having Basie ride his horse of perfect time
Like an avenging angel over top volume,
Hoisting scotch and milk as he galloped
Into Tillie's ear, headlong down her throat
To roar all night in her sulfurous organs.

SITTING WITH LESTER YOUNG

If you want to see Lester Young,
Dusk must become your light,
So Zimmer sits beside him at
His window in the Alvin Hotel.

Pres is blue beyond redemption.
His tenor idle on the table,
He looks down at the street,
Drinking his gin and port.
Buildings slice the last light
From the day.
                    If Pres could
Shuffle into a club again like
A wounded animal, he would
Blow his ultimate melancholy,
But nights belong to others now.

Zimmer can only watch Lester
In the half light of his sadness,
Old whispers slipping around,
Words into melodies,
As holy silence means the most.

ZIMMER AND THE GIANT FRENCH GOAT

"Near Lyon they talk of cloning super goats."
~UPI

Two massive, crescent steeples
Curve toward each other
Under ocher wisps of sky
Above a tree-lined ridge.

"Horns of the goat," Marcel says,
So grim in his perplexity. "You see,
Zimmer~it has grown even more."

Together we walk from town
Past shuttered, gray stone houses,
Past the *marie* and *bureau de poste*,
The *boucherie*, *boulangerie*.

Into harvested fields we shamble
Past stacks of winter cordwood,
Ducks and geese in their mesh;
Marcel with his crooked stick,
I in my jeans and baseball cap,
Past bulls and mincing cows,
Pens of hunt dogs belling,
Up to the rise and over.

There stands the giant goat
Astride a saddleback hummock,
Ranting and peeing sallow rivers,
Tall as the Eiffel, wide as a *chateau*;
Her nostrils boggy and eyes askew
As she gnashes on a rusty tractor.

Hip deep in a pool of whey, Marcel

Is grunting and shaking his head.
"*Mon ami,* now you observe,
In France all goats are but one goat.
Where once there were millions,
Now there is this *bique Amazonian,*
La nounou primordial, *la chèvre géant,*
One beast for all our cheese."

ZIMMER DIRECTING UNIVERSITY PRESSES

"The most unfortunate sort of misfortune is once
to have been happy."
~Boethius

It was like being birds in high feather,
We gathered twigs and mud,
As we learned to fetch and tuck.
We sat on nests of our weavings,
Laying eggs one at a time,
Month after month, year upon year.
Three decades passed like thirty
Pensive taps on the inside of a shell.

Our children hatched singing,
Impossibly beautiful, so well attended,
So rare and rarely appreciated.
Though large birds rasped and
Feinted, we held our space and sang.

But the brains of birds are small;
There is room for only one emotion.
For a long time I was blithe;
But one day storms slashed down
And split us into twittering factions.
I became a low bird, my breath short,
Tail drooped, plumage blasted and dull.
The other birds tried to forget me.

That year just before snow fell,
I woke to find my flock had flown away,
Riding evening zephyrs to desert me,
Leaving me only with memories of perfidy,

And the whole, long winter to be endured.
Now I have grown hoary like an old,
Bleached aviary~dizzy as if I might
Warp and fall apart at any moment.

If I have learned one useful thing:
It is that earth is indifferent~
Despite its pleasing illusions
Of birth, flight, and work~it never
Regarded me as more important
Than haunted deer in the flurries,
Than furry scats of coyotes,
Stripped trees, or mice that stitch
The drifts with nervous tracks.

ZIMMER STUNNED BY RANCOR

"Dear Zimmer," the letter said,
"I have spent ten years
Hating your guts; but now,
After much consideration,
After therapy and medication,
Surgery and divorce,
I forgive you for rejecting me."

Zimmer wrings his sweaty hands,
Having been forgiven without
Knowing he had sinned.

"What have I done?" he thinks.
"Have I made evil choices?"

A whole decade of secret malevolence!
No wonder my teeth ached,
My asthma foamed up,
My vision was ambiguous,
My heart staggered and flopped
Against the inside of my ribs.

WHAT ZIMMER WILL DO

The earliest color photographs were called autochromes (1904-1930), formed on glass plates using a layer of minute grains of starch dyed red, green, and blue and coated with a panchromatic emulsion. When viewed closely, the finished images are like miniature Pointillist paintings.

I am looking at an image of two young French women sitting
        in a garden around 1906,
and I become the great bird of love again;
crazy with spring, I swoop down
into the middle of the *belle époque*,
skitter and flop on a gravel path at the feet
of these two unsmiling French girls who sit
with their hair pulled back over eyes of shade.

I will make them blush and laugh
in their pink, summer frocks as I fly up
and dart between their wicker chairs
over beds of primroses, fan plants
and columbines, to an open window
where picnic hampers have been placed.

Then the three of us will ramble
Into sunlight and droning grasses.
I will circle their lovely, oval heads,
Gently plucking at their barrettes until
They laugh, "Zimmer, *l'oiseau absurde!*"
You crazy bird! And toss me
Bits of bread and boiled egg.

Zimmer in Autumn

Birds and leaves disconnect in autumn,
But I hang on.
                    Not one flower
Has to open for my happiness.

I am content in this season
Of retreat, finished with growth,
With striving and sorting.

I do not want even one cell
To stir and split.
Let it all stand as it is.

Zimmer Imagines Heaven

I sit with Joseph Conrad in Monet's garden.
We are listening to Yeats chant his poems.
A breeze stirs through Thomas Hardy's moustache,
John Skelton has gone to the house for beer,
Wanda Landowska lightly fingers a harpsichord.
Along the spruce tree walk Roberto Clemente and
Thurman Munson whistle a baseball back and forth.
Mozart chats with Ellington in the roses.

Monet smokes and dabs his canvas in the sun,
Brueghel and Turner set easels behind the wisteria.
The band is warming up in the Big Studio:
Bean, Brute, Bird and Serge on saxes,
Kai, Bill Harris, Lawrence Brown, trombones,
Little Jazz, Clifford, Diz on trumpets,
Klook plays drums, Mingus bass, Bud the piano.

Later Madam Schumann-Heink will sing Schubert,
The monks of Benedictine Abbey will chant.
There will be more poems from Emily Dickinson,
James Wright, John Clare, Walt Whitman.
Shakespeare rehearses players for *King Lear*.

At dusk Alice Toklas brings out platters
Of sweetbreads *á la Napolitaine, Salad Livoniére*,
And a tureen of Gaspacho of Malaga.
After the meal Brahms passes fine cigars.
God comes then, radiant with a bottle of cognac
She pours generously into the snifters.
I tell Her I have begun to learn what
Heaven is about. She wants to hear.
It is, I say, being thankful for eternity.
Her smile is the best part of the day.

Paul Zimmer has published twelve books of poetry, including *Family Reunion* (University of Pittsburgh Press), which won an Award for Literature from the Academy and Institute of Arts and Letters; *The Great Bird of Love* (University of Illinois Press), which was selected by William Stafford for the National Poetry Series; *Big Blue Train* (University of Arkansas Press) and *Crossing to Sunlight: Selected Poems* (University of Georgia Press). He has published two books of his memoirs and essays, *After the Fire: A Writer Finds His Place* (University of Minnesota Press) and *Trains in the Distance* (Kent State University Press). His writing has been awarded six Pushcart Prizes, three for poetry and three for prose. His pieces have been named as Notable Essays five times in the annual Best Essays of the Year series, and in 2005 he won *Shenandoah's* Thomas H. Carter Prize for the Essay.

Over the past thirty-five years he has read his poems at more than three hundred colleges and poetry centers from coast to coast. He has recorded his poems for the Library of Congress and was twice awarded writing fellowships from the National Endowment for the Arts. His poems have been widely anthologized, most recently in Garrison Keillor's *Good Poems* and *Poetry 180*, edited by Billy Collins. For thirty years he worked as a scholarly publisher and was founding editor of three ongoing book series at university presses--Pittsburgh, Georgia and Iowa--and initiated The Flannery O'Connor Award Series at the University of Georgia Press. He has been poet-in-residence for periods of time at the University of Montana, Hollins University, Chico State University, Wichita State University, the University of Tennessee (2009) and Appalachian State University (2009). He now lives on a farm in Wisconsin and spends part of each year in the south of France.